Wineucation the Cookbook

Jennifer McDonald

ISBN: 978-1-952263-54-5

Dedication

I want to dedicate this book to my loving parents, who taught me the importance of living fearlessly and gratefully. I also dedicate this to my supportive husband and two children, whom I love to the moon and back.

Acknowledgment

I would not have articulated this book without the participation, membership, and fellowship from the Wineucation class attendees over the past several years in Wichita. The Wineucation attendees tried these recipes and food pairings and provided valuable feedback and insight. They helped me push through to establish Jenny Dawn Cellars.

I also want to acknowledge the hardworking former and current Jenny Dawn Cellars team members who helped prepare these delicious dishes for us to gorge on. I gained plenty of inspiration from their food crafting skills in preparing mouth-watering dishes perfect for wine pairing.

About the Author

Jennifer McDonald is a successful winemaker, entrepreneur, human resources, and recruiting professional. She has executed several strategic initiatives for some of the largest employers residing in Wichita, KS. She leveraged her business acumen and leadership skills to venture into the world of wine. She became the Founder, CEO, and Winemaker at Jenny Dawn Cellars in 2016. Since its establishment, she has celebrated the art and science of wine. She has helped hundreds of people connect with each other by creating special moments through the celebration of wine.

Jennifer took college chemistry through a local college and winemaking courses through US Davis online to excel and improve in winemaking. She also has a Master's degree in Agribusiness from Kansas State University. She utilized her degree to research and prepare data for consumer wine preferences. She began her journey in the winemaking business by first preparing wine at home.

As a home winemaker, she bottled savory red wines and light and crisp white wines all prepared from her kitchen or basement. She ended up winning medals for her delicious creations. Her made-at-home wines received a gold, three silvers, and two bronze medals from the Kansas Winemakers and Grape Growers Association. Now, her boutique winery consists of a production area and tasting room, which can transform into a gorgeous event venue. Jennifer also teaches a monthly wine class called Wineucation.

She is married to her husband, Matthew, and has two children, Desmond and Emma, who have always inspired her to pursue her passions. Her love for food grew by preparing delicious meals at home, which she began to pair with her marvelous wines.

Preface

Food is celebrated everywhere, regardless of ethnicity, culture, or religion; every human gracing this planet adores food one way or another. After feasting on dishes filled with beef, cheese, and all that savory goodness, you just can't pass up the opportunity for a plate of dessert. That is magical in itself, but nothing beats food paired with the right wine.

This cookbook accumulates 27 recipes ranging from beef dishes to vegan enchiladas, to celebrate the art of food. It includes dishes completely different from each other, yet powerful enough to bring families together. The best part of it all is that these dishes taste extravagant when paired with the correct Jenny Dawn Cellar wine! This book is packed with not only food but knowledge regarding what wine pairing complements which dish.

It will broaden your perspective of wine, allowing you to improve your palate and savor wine with food like you have not experienced before. It will help you choose the right wine for the right dish. So, when you are choosing a heavy, meaty dish with strips of oil-glazed vegetables, you will know whether velvety red wine or sparkling white wine is the right fit.

Contents

Page Left Blank Intentionally

Introduction

Paired with a glass of Jenny Dawn Cellars wine, the savory and sweet dishes in this book will send your taste buds on a ride of delight. The 27 recipes in here are not only nutritious but also flavorful. They are dripping with cheese and are fragrant with seasonings. They give you delicious, vegetable-rich, as well as tasty meat options – all to indulge the diversity of your palate!

You will find dishes of every kind here all stacked in one place. You can select Smoked Trout Pate or Spiced Poached Pears. There's Beef Carpaccio, but there's also Vegan Enchiladas. Take your pick. These recipes will come in handy on every occasion and event. The best part of them all is that they are not time-consuming and include general ingredients that can be found in any grocery store near you.

Food is more than just a source of nutrition. It is more than something that quietens our grumbling stomachs. Food is also a way of bringing people together, just like Jenny Dawn Cellars wine. You cook on festive days like Christmas or Thanksgiving. And so, food helps you celebrate and strengthen the bond you have with your family and friends.

Food is also one way to showcase diversity. The food on your plate is not what someone on the other side of the world eats. Even if we do not speak the same language, food from varying cultures connects us: it helps us communicate through the language of flavor. Some dishes I have included in this recipe book came to life because different cultures met one another and turned food into a more globalized experience.

Food also comforts us. It is a storehouse of warm memories. Your mom's homemade chocolate chip cookies, that tub of ice cream you always shared with your high school best friend, and the casseroles your nana baked for you… can you recall the experience and did the food cheer you up?

Food releases chemicals like dopamine, which keeps you content and joyful. It stabilizes your mental health. If you want, food can be your companion when you are stressed or down in the dumps. If you think about it, you will be impressed by how much food can do for you!

As I worked through this cookbook, I included recipes that I have served during our Wineucation classes. I also chose recipes that are close to my heart because of how well they pair with wine. A good portion of the recipes in this book include meats of all kinds. The desserts here are packed with berries and a generous amount of cream cheese.

The best part of it all is that I developed these recipes keeping wine in mind. Wine offers a unique mix of flavor that not only enhances everything you taste but also helps with digestion. It also improves blood circulation and works as a great stress-reliever. We call wine the 'Nectar of Gods.' Its unparalleled ability to intensify the flavor of a meal keeps things interesting.

This is also why I pursued a career in the wine industry. I spent 12 years working in Corporate Human Resources and Recruiting before becoming a winemaker, wine connoisseur, and food enthusiast. My passion for business and the skills I learned through the years of hustling in the corporate world helped me establish myself in the wine industry. I realized that I had a love for wine and its distinctive ability to bring people together. It took me five years, but I was able to turn my passion for wine into a career by opening an urban winery in downtown Wichita, KS.

Wine changed my life in unimaginable ways, and I want to share with the world all that it offers. This is the reason why I wrote this book. Once you learn the right wine to pair with the right food, you will not be able to stop. You will want to learn more and more about how you can open the doors of taste-heaven for yourself!

The food that you eat can change the way you taste wine, too. The way we prepare a dish gives clues to what wine might go well with it. The point of this recipe book is to give you 27 mouth-watering recipes that, once paired with Jenny Dawn Cellars wine, have the perfect harmony to create a burst of flavor in your mouth.

As you proceed with this recipe book, you will realize how wine can act as a spice while you are eating. Once you choose the right combination, you can enhance the subtle characteristics of your meal. You can match the intensity and flavors to your palate's liking and witness the many ways in which wine affects the taste of each dish differently. This realization about wine pushed me to compile these recipes. Everyone, regardless of being a wine lover or not, needs to try the wonderful 'spice' that is wine.

The Art of Pairing Wine with Food

When you pair wine with food, you need to make sure

that one does not overpower the other. Once you drink wine while eating, you will notice a change in the flavor of the wine as well as the meal. Therefore, it is vital to strike a balance. For example, you should pair light-bodied wines with lighter foods and full-bodied wines with richer or fatter options. Let's dive more into the different flavors and how wine can affect them:

Sweet – If the food is high in sugar, it gives the wine a drier taste. It ends up tasting a bit more acidic and bitter. If you choose a sweeter wine, it can help balance the sweetness of the meal and not diminish the wine's fruity and full taste.

Savory – Though it is a primary flavor; it can be hard to find the right wine for savory dishes. The reason is that the level of salt in each savory food can be different. This ultimately affects whether the wine would taste sweet or bitter. You must pick a wine according to the salt-level. Acidic wine goes well with high salt-levels, while fruity wine complements low salt-levels.

Acidic Foods – Foods with higher levels of acidity tend to make the wine taste richer and more flavorful. Being paired with such food reduces the acidic levels of the wine and boosts the fruitfulness of the beverage. Once again, you need to balance out the meal and wine. Pair acidic wine with foods that are higher in acidic content. Never sip on low-acidic wine while consuming a meal with high acidic content. Try experimenting with this and compare the flavor of wine with each meal. It will help you grasp the idea of how wine alters and adjusts according to the taste and acidic content of each food.

Apart from the flavor of a meal, the way it is prepared matters as well. I consider poached or steamed food as delicate, so the wine you pair with it needs to be delicate as well to attain the perfect balance. If you are dealing with a rather complex recipe, try to match it with a wine that has a strong flavor.

Just remember rules are meant to be broken, so don't be afraid of experimenting. This recipe book is here to help you venture into the world of wine pairing. I have developed these recipes to complement my Jenny Dawn Cellars wine, but it will also open your eyes to the way the bitterness, acidity, and sweetness of food changes the taste of wine, which, in turn, changes the way your food tastes. So, go ahead and try them. I invite you to dive deeper into the art that is food and wine!

Recipe List

Here is the complete list of the recipes included in this cookbook:

Beef

- Rosemary Roast Beef
- Beef and Goat Cheese Crostini
- Mini Beef Wellingtons
- Beef Carpaccio
- Grill Skirt Steak and Peaches

Poultry and Pork

- Strawberry Chicken Salad
- Honey Basil Chicken Sliders
- Tarragon & Whole Grain Mustard Stuffed Chicken Breast
- Garlic and Herb Roasted Pork Tenderloin
- Chicken Scampi Pasta

Seafood

- Smoked Trout Pate
- Broiled Scallops with Parmesan Crust
- Smoked Salmon Vol Au Vents
- Grilled Salmon Salad with Sherry-Honey Vinaigrette
- Crab and Asparagus Salad

- Campanella al Forno

Sides and Dressings

- Skillet Green Beans and Potatoes
- Goat Cheese Stuffed Figs
- Honey Balsamic Vinaigrette
- Parmesan Salad Dressing
- Shaved Fennel and Avocado Salad
- Grilled Portobello Mushrooms

Desserts

- Spiced Poached Pears
- Lemon Blueberry Clafoutis
- Honey Soaked Figs.
- Strawberry Balsamic Crostini

Vegan

- Vegan Enchiladas

Chapter 1
Beef

Beef is a delicacy preferred over other red and white meat because of the extraordinary flavor it offers and its nutritional benefit. It can be prepared in several ways – so it is very versatile! Another reason beef is great is that it has some exceptional health benefits.

Red meat is packed with iron that is quickly and easily absorbed by the body. When it comes to protein, beef wins out over other red meat as well. It is also richer in zinc and other necessary vitamins like riboflavin, vitamins B6, and B12. It also contains huge amounts of L-Carnitine, a compound important for the internal functions of our body.

This compound can also reduce the risks of developing diabetes and can even help with weight loss, which goes against the general stereotypes about beef. On top of these benefits, one of the most special qualities of beef is that it pairs amazingly well with red wine! The main reason behind this is that red wine comprises of tannins. We find tannins in grape seeds, skin, and even in wine barrels. When the protein in beef combines with tannins, it creates a harmony of flavors. So, as you go to restaurants and order wine, the waiter would always recommend a beef dish. The tannin molecules soften the meat, which helps make it more flavorful. The softened fat in the meat then makes the wine taste even smoother with a fruity taste.

The qualities of the meat and wine easily balance each other out, hence creating the famous trend of teaming up beef with a glass of red wine. So whether it's about pairing Rosemary Roast Beef with a bottle of Jenny Dawn Cellars Cabernet Sauvignon, or even enjoying a Grill Skirt Steak and Peaches with a glass of Pinot Noir, these red meat recipes and pairings will have you asking, "Where's the beef and the wine?"

Recipes
Rosemary Roast Beef

Pairs with Cabernet Sauvignon or Black Locomotive
Serves 6

Ingredients

- Boneless roast – 3 lbs

- Fresh rosemary – ¼ cup
- Garlic cloves - ¼ cup
- Sea salt – to taste
- Ground black pepper - to taste
- Olive oil – 4 tbsp
- Butter – 4 tbsp
- Mushrooms – 4 cups
- Beef stock – 1 cup

Directions

- Preheat oven to 350F.
- Season the roast with salt and pepper in a separate dish.
- Warm the skillet on medium heat and moisten it with olive oil. Place the meat in the skillet and cook.
- Mix two tablespoons of oil, garlic, and rosemary in a bowl.
- Rub the mixture properly on the beef. Then, pop the roasted beef in the oven for a good hour or more as needed.
- Before removing the roast from the oven, cook the diced mushrooms with butter in a pan. Put the mushrooms aside on a plate.
- Add beef stock to the pan and heat it till it thickens. Add the mushrooms and mix in some butter. Stir the mixture well, and pour the sauce onto the roast.
- Serve hot!

Beef and Goat Cheese Crostini

Pairs with Pinot Noir
Serves 8

Ingredients

- Baguette ¼ inch slices – ½ cup
- Olive oil – 4 tbsp
- Garlic – 5 pieces from a clove
- Beef tenderloin – 14 ounces
- Sea salt – to taste
- Black pepper – to taste
- Basil pesto – 1/3 cup

Ingredients to prepare the cheese:

- Cream cheese – 4 ounces
- Goat cheese – 4 ounces
- Olive oil – 2 tbsp
- Red pepper flakes – ½ tsp
- Sea salt – to taste

Directions

- Mix oil and garlic cloves, then brush the contents onto baguette slices.
- Place the slices on a baking sheet and under a broiler for a couple of minutes.
- Drizzle olive oil on a pan, and chop garlic cloves into the pan. Saute the cloves for two minutes or until they turn light brown.
- Season the steak with salt and pepper, and cook it in the pan for 5 minutes.
- Settle the meet on a nearby table and prepare the goat cheese by mixing all ingredients through the help of a mixer.
- Cut the beef into slices and rest it onto the baguette coated with goat cheese.
- Serve.

Mini Beef Wellingtons

Pairs with Cabernet Sauvignon or Black Locomotive
Serves 8

Ingredients

- Olive oil – 2 tbsps
- Beef tenderloin – 2 lbs cut into 24 (1-inch) cubes
- Sea salt – to taste
- Black pepper – to taste
- Mushrooms – 10 ounces
- Shallot – 1
- Puff pastry, thawed – 2 sheets

Directions

- Preheat the oven to 400 degrees.
- Cut the beef into cubes and season it with salt and pepper.

- Spread oil on a skillet. Cook the meat for a couple of minutes. Let it rest on the side.
- Cook the mushrooms till they're juicy. Then, dice and add the shallot. Saute for 7-10 minutes.
- Take out the puff pastry and place it onto a baking sheet with parchment paper.
- Roll up a pastry to a 10-14 inch rectangle. Put the shallot and mushroom mixture on the pastry, spacing it in rows.
- Add in the cooked beef. Cut the pastry into squares. Close off both sides of the pastry by folding them neatly.
- Place the packets seam down and press them to shut the pastry completely. Settle the dish in the oven for about 23-25 minutes.
- Serve.

Beef Carpaccio

Pairs with Pinot Noir
Serves 4

Ingredients

- Beef fillet – 14 ounces
- Arugula – 2
- Parmesan – 1 tbsp
- Sea salt – to taste
- Black pepper – to taste

Directions

- Place a parchment paper on the kitchen slab.
- Cut the beef into slices. Take each slice and place it onto the paper and top it with another parchment paper.
- Pound the beef till its flattened.

- Place the arugula on a plate and take out the beef slices, decorating them as per your liking.
- Top it all off with seasoning and parmesan.
- Serve.

Lemon Olive Oil Dressing

Ingredients

- Lemon juice – 6 tbsp
- Sea salt – ½ tsp
- Black pepper – ¼ tsp
- Garlic– 1
- Olive oil – ½ cup

Directions

- Mince the garlic thoroughly and place all the ingredients in a jar.
- Combine them by carefully shaking the mixture.

Grill Skirt Steak and Peaches

Pairs with Pinot Noir

Ingredients

- Garlic cloves – 2
- Bay leaf – 1
- Small shallot – 1
- Jalapeno – 1
- Zest and juice of 1 lemon
- Soy sauce – 2 tbsp
- Thyme – ½ tsp
- Canola oil – 1 cup and 1 tbsp
- Salt – to taste
- Ground pepper – to taste
- Skirt steak – 1 ½ pound cut into 4 pieces
- Dijon mustard – 1 tbsp

- Boiling water – ½ cup
- Honey – 2 tbsp
- Cinnamon – ½ tsp
- Ginger – 1 ½ tsp
- Peaches – 4

Directions

- Place the bay leaf, shallot, lemon juice, soy sauce, chopped thyme, and lemon zest in a blender. Blend the ingredients to perfection.
- Add half a cup of oil and keep the blender on till the mixture is smooth.
- Sprinkle seasoning on the mixture. Pour some of it onto a baking dish and place the steak on top of it.
- Spread some more of the mixture on the steak, and let it rest for 20 minutes.
- Add Dijon mustard to the rest of the mixture, and blend it all.
- Take a pot, add honey, grated ginger, and cinnamon into it. Mix it all well. Pour it into a medium-sized bowl along with the remaining ingredients.
- Remove the rest of the marinade from the skirt steak. Season the meat and grill it for 6 to 8 minutes.
- Grill the peach halves for 8 minutes, until they are charred and slightly squishy.
- With a sharp knife, slice the steak and carefully make wedges out of the peaches.
- Serve along with the dressing.

Chapter 2
Poultry and Pork

Pork is well-known for its versatility. It can be prepared in numerous ways and still satisfy your taste buds. You can roast it for a crisp and crunchy texture, spice it up with different seasonings, and indulge in its meaty goodness. If you prefer soft, tender, and juicy meat, then whipping up some braised pork belly is the easiest route to take.

Pork's versatility reaches a new height once you consider different pork joints. As you prepare each joint, you'll notice the apparent change in taste. Lather a shoulder joint with seasonings, put cheese on the side, and notice the richness of the meat. A roasted pork leg will surprise you with a crunch. Every joint can provide you a mouth-watering taste and fulfill your craving.

Even though some people consider pork to be unhealthy, it is nourishing if prepared in less oil and saturated fat. Pork is high in selenium, which is a trace mineral and a beneficial antioxidant that reduces the risk of heart diseases. It even helps with improving memory. Pork is also rich in zinc, ensuring the immune function works fine. It is an amazing source of vitamin B12 and vitamin B6, which keeps the blood cells healthy and helps in red blood cell formation, respectively. When it comes to popularity, pork does seem to dominate the charts. Pork has taken over the world because of its flexible ways of preparation, and delicious taste. It is craved to the point that pork has replaced beef as the popular meat in numerous countries, especially in North America. Bacon has played a major part in increasing pork's demand.

Breakfast in a lot of American households consists of eggs, sunny side up, and a few strips of bacon. You can find bacon in every fast-food chain, even topping French fries. Many restaurants include bacon-related dishes on the menu to attract new customers.

All these traits are enough to prove pork is a crowd-pleaser, but its exceptional qualities do not end there. Pork also tastes mind-blowing when paired with the right wine and cooked at the right temperature. Pork is truly diverse and can be prepared in various flavorful ways. So, the way it is cooked will determine which wine will taste special with it. Generally, pork tends to be light with a hint of sweetness, so it goes well with medium-bodied red wines such as Pinot Noir or light crisp wines such as Chardonnay. Overall, choosing a specific wine would depend on the taste and texture of the pork dish. Chicken meat is just as impressive as pork. It is a type of meat that has the entire world wrapped around its delicate flavor. It is easy and quick to prepare. Even if you spend just 20-30 minutes preparing a chicken dish, it will still turn out to be a masterpiece. The reason is that chicken does not require any precision when cooked, while beef and pork ensure to take their sweet time to become tender and juicy.

Chicken can be incorporated into any dish and enhance its flavor. Plain white rice with vegetables can transform into a magnificent dish just with the addition of chicken. Vegetable soup can turn extra flavorful when shredded chicken is added.

Chicken can be smoked, fried, and grilled, just like any other meat. It also complements almost every seasoning, spice, and cooking method that exists. Unless you burn the meat, you cannot go wrong with chicken. It is also more nutritious than other meats and even included in weight-losing recipes because it has a lower fat content. It has minerals like phosphorus, iron, and selenium. Chicken is also low in saturated fat, which is responsible for high blood pressure and high cholesterol levels, as it is lean meat. As for wine pairing for chicken, generally, white wines such as Chardonnay are a great match. Red wines such as a Sweet Red Wine also work, depending on the recipe and method of cooking. This does not mean that you can't include rosé wines because they complement spicy-flavored chicken dishes quite well.

If you are pairing roasted chicken with a glass of wine, then opting for a light white wine or rosé wines are the best option because of the tender meat. All in all, white wine is the ultimate partner for chicken dishes. Choosing a white wine with the correct texture and weight will bring out the essence of the lean meat, leaving you yearning for more.

Before beginning to cook, grab a glass of wine to set yourself in the right mood. Pour your Jenny Dawn Cellars wine in your glass. These chicken and pork recipes will complete that glass of wine. From a family favorite of Garlic and Herb Roasted Pork Tenderloin to the crowd-pleasing Honey Basil Chicken Sliders, the only question people will be asking you is if they can have more!

Recipes
Strawberry Chicken Salad

Pairs with Red Caboose
Serves 4

Ingredients

- Chicken breast – 4 pieces
- Romaine Lettuce – 4 cups
- Sliced strawberries – 1 cup
- Cubed goat cheese – 8 tbsp
- Sea salt – to taste
- Black pepper – to taste
- Honey balsamic vinaigrette – 4 ounces

Directions

- Season grilled chicken.

- Heat a saucepan or skillet on medium-high heat.
- Add olive oil and cook the chicken for about 5-7 minutes.
- Slice the chicken into thin slices.
- Build the salad by mixing, strawberries, lettuce, and goat cheese.
- Add chicken.
- Drizzle honey balsamic vinaigrette over each salad and serve.

Honey Basil Chicken Sliders

Pairs with Chardonnay or Union Station
Serves 6

Ingredients

- Chicken breasts – 2
- Slider buns – 12
- Basil pesto jar – 1 of 8.1 ounces
- Honey – 4 tbsp
- Tomatoes – 2
- Mozzarella cheese – 1 cup

Directions

- Preheat the oven to 350 degrees.
- Split the buns in half and spread the shredded chicken on the bottom layer and place tomatoes on the top.
- In a bowl, mix your pesto and honey, spread it over the chicken, reserving a tbsp or two.
- Sprinkle with cheese and top with another half of slider buns. Brush the top with pesto mixture.
- Cover and bake for 25 minutes.

Tarragon & Whole Grain Mustard Stuffed Chicken Breast

Pairs with Chardonnay or Union Station

Ingredients

- Chicken airline breast with skin – 4
- Mustard – 4 tbsp

- Tarragon – 1
- Shallot– 1
- Olive oil – 1 tbsp
- Canola oil – 1 tbsp
- Salt and pepper – to taste.

Directions

- Preheat the oven to 400 degrees.
- Take a bowl and add mustard, chopped shallots and tarragon, and olive oil. Mix all the ingredients.
- Now, to stuff the filling in the chicken, use your fingers to make a small pocket at the top.
- Place one tbsp of filling in the gap for each chicken breast.
- In a pan containing canola oil, cook the seasoned chicken breast for about 10 minutes. Do the same for the other side as well.
- Serve.

Garlic and Herb Roasted Pork Tenderloin

Pairs with Pinot Noir
Serves 4 to 6 people

Ingredients

- Pork tenderloins – 2 lbs
- Salt and pepper – to taste
- Rosemary stalks– 2
- Thyme – 2
- Garlic cloves, peeled – 6 to 8
- Zest of one lemon.
- Olive oil – ¼ cup
- Beer or white wine – ½ cup

Direction

- Dry the tenderloins and season with salt and pepper.

- Put the meat on a baking pan, and then preheat the oven to 475 degrees.
- Take the leaves of the rosemary stalks and thyme and add them in a blender. Also, add in the cloves and lemon zest.
- Keep the blender running and splash some olive oil in the mixture. Make sure the mixture has a similar texture to that of a smooth paste.
- Lather the meat with the paste, and pop the tenderloins into the oven for 10 minutes.
- Flip the tenderloins and place them back into the oven for 10 minutes. Make sure the meat is not overcooked; keep checking when the temperature hits 155 degrees.
- Heat a pan and pour alcohol – beer or white wine.
- Let the mixture simmer so it can turn into a thick and rich sauce.
- Slice the meat, pour the sauce on top, and serve.

Chicken Scampi Pasta

Pairs with Chardonnay or Union Station
Serves 4

Ingredients

- Linguine – 8 ounces
- Red pepper flakes – 1 tsp
- Cajun seasoning – 1 tsp
- Olive oil – 1 tbsp
- Chardonnay – ¼ cup
- Lemon juice – ¼ cup
- Salted butter – 4 tbsp
- Shrimp– 1 pound

- Garlic cloves - 6
- Sea salt – to taste
- Black pepper – to taste
- Zest of 1 lemon
- Parsley leaves – 2 tbsp
- Parmesan cheese– 1 cup

Directions

- Prepare pasta as per the instructions on the packet. Then heat up a skillet and add in butter.
- Crush the red pepper flakes, and them in the skillet along with Cajun seasoning, oil, shrimp, and chopped garlic.
- Cook for a couple of minutes, then add the wine and lemon juice. Sprinkle the seasoning on top.
- Turn the heat off and add pasta to the mix. Also, add in the zest and about half a cup of parmesan. Mix all the ingredients well.
- Sprinkle the rest of the parmesan along with parsley on top.
- Serve.

Chapter 3
Seafood

Seafood is a great contender for red meat and lean meat because of its numerous health benefits and diversity. It is always refreshing and light on the stomach with a fresh smell and a delicate taste.

One great quality of seafood is that it is loved and consumed all over the world. While there are countries that ban specific kinds of meat because of religious or cultural purposes, seafood is generally consumed in almost every country. This is also why it has evolved so much.

Seafood is also great for feasts, celebrations, and impressing your guests. There are so many ways of preparing seafood. For example, you can whip up a creamy shrimp pasta but also make salmon sushi – both opposite dishes.

Seafood is also loaded with nutrition and minerals. The reason why people lean more toward seafood, in general, is because of its abundant health benefits. Seafood is rich in omega-3, which is necessary for preventing heart diseases.

Seafood consists of low levels of saturated fat than other meat options and is considered as a source of healthy protein. The protein is also easier on the digestive system. It is also low in calories and high in minerals and vitamins. Some of these vitamins include B-complex vitamins, vitamin D, and vitamin A, responsible for various healthy functions, including strengthening the bones and muscles and improving vision. Seafood also helps improve your skin and prevents the development of irritating skin conditions. The reason is that seafood is packed with omega-3 fatty acids, which keep the skin moisturized and protected from UV rays of the sun.

Regardless of how nutritious and universal seafood might be, it would not taste the best if it is paired with the wrong wine. If you are going for a fried seafood dish, the best option is a sparkling wine or rosé as it does not diminish the taste of the wine like other wines paired with fried foods. If you are going for salmon, enjoying it with a not-so-tannic red wine such as Pinot Noir is perfect. Light flaky fish complements white wine like Sauvignon Blanc and Chardonnay. And if you have chosen a salty dish like a fish with a strong sea-salt flavor, it is better to pair it with a wine that can withstand the salt, and not get overpowered by it. Now, all you must do is lean back, and grab your Jenny Dawn Cellars wine, prepare these meals, and pour yourself a glass of the wines I've mentioned complement each recipe.

As they say, 'If you teach a person how to fish, you feed them for a lifetime.' The only issue here is that you are not including a refreshing glass of white, red, rosé, or sparkling wine to complete the picture. Whether you're passing out Smoked Salmon Vol Au Vents to go alongside a bottle of Jenny Dawn Cellars Chardonnay or enjoying a candlelit dinner featuring my Grilled Salmon Salad with Sherry-Honey Vinaigrette Salad with a glass of Jenny Dawn Cellars Pinot Noir, self-caught or store-bought, these seafood recipes are sure to let you live in the moment.

Recipes
Smoked Trout Pate

Pairs with Chardonnay and Union Station
Serves 4

Ingredients

- Cream cheese– 4 ounces
- Shallot – 2 tbsp
- Lemon juice – 1 tbsp
- Chives – 1 tbsp
- Flaked smoked trout – 2 ½ ounces
- Sea salt – to taste
- Baguette slices

Directions

- Dice the shallots into tiny pieces, chop the chives and add them both in a bowl with cream cheese and lemon juice.
- Mix it all till the mixture becomes smooth. Season with salt and fold in trout.
- Serve with slices on the side.

Broiled Scallops with Parmesan Crust

Pairs with Red Caboose

Serves 6

Ingredients

- Sea Scallops – 2 lbs
- Butter – 2 tbsp
- Olive oil – 2 tbsp
- Bread crumbs – ½ cup
- Parmesan cheese – 2 tbsp
- Parsley finely chopped – 1 tsp
- Paprika – ¼ tsp
- Black pepper – to taste

Directions

- Preheat oven.
- Dry the sea scallops and place them in a bowl.
- Add in olive oil and melted butter, mixing it all thoroughly.
- Pour the mixture over the scallops.
- Take the rest of the ingredients and place them in a separate bowl. Then, add in the scallops.
- After coating the scallops in bread crumbs, place them on the top rack of the oven for 10 minutes.
- Serve.

Smoked Salmon Vol Au Vents

Pairs with Chardonnay and Union Station

Makes 9 Pieces

Ingredients

- Puff pastry – 1 sheet
- Cream cheese – 6 tbsp
- Mustard – 1 ½ tsp
- Minced chives – 1 tbsp
- Slices of smoked salmon– 5
- Egg – 1

Directions

- Preheat the oven to 400 degrees.

- Spread the pastry on a floured surface, and take a cookie-cutter to cut out circles.
- On top of the cookie-cutter, put a wire rack to ensure the cookies are equal in size.
- Bake for 10-25 minutes.
- Add the chives, cream cheese, and mustard in a bowl and mix well.
- Fill the top of the golden-brown pastry, cut a hole at the top to fill it with the cream cheese mixture.
- Serve.

Grilled Salmon Salad with Sherry-Honey Vinaigrette Salad

Pairs with Pinot Noir

Ingredients

- Salmon fillets with skin – 4-5 ounces
- Canola oil – 1 tsp
- Haricot verts – 6 ounces
- Baby potatoes – 8 ounces
- Baby gold or Chioggia beets – 1 bunch
- Arugula – 3 ounces
- Slices bacon – 4
- Extra-virgin olive oil – 1 tbsp
- Water – ¼ cup

Directions

- Preheat oven to 350 degrees.

- Pour water and oil in a baking dish and add beets into it. Cover and cook in the oven for an hour. After removing it from the oven, peel off the skin from the beets.
- Add a tablespoon of salt and water in a big pot with potatoes. Place it on the stove to boil for at least 15 minutes. Make sure the potatoes are soft before removing from heat.
- Place the haricot verts in a pot and heat for a couple of minutes. Set it aside.
- Heat a pan and cook a lightly salted fish with canola oil. Season the flesh and continue to cook for a couple of minutes till the skin becomes crispy. Flip the fish and cook for a few more minutes.
- Then, crisp bacon in a pan and crumble it into pieces in a bowl.
- Season the potatoes, beets, arugula, haricot verts with salt and pepper. Then drizzle vinaigrette on each.
- Place the arugula on a plate, and add potatoes, bacon pieces, salmon, beets, and haricot verts on the top.
- Serve.

Vinaigrette

Ingredients

- Extra virgin olive oil – ¼ cup
- Honey – 2 tbsp
- Canola oil – ¼ cup
- Mustard – 2 tbsp
- Aged sherry vinegar – 3 tbsp
- Salt – ½ tsp

Directions

- Mix honey, mustard, salt, and vinegar in a bowl.
- Drizzle oil in the bowl while mixing quickly and powerfully.
- Enjoy!

Crab and Asparagus Salad

Pairs with Chardonnay

Ingredients

- Asparagus, trimmed – 2 pounds
- Chopped chives – ½ cup 2 tbsp
- Butter leaf lettuce – 1
- Navel oranges – 2
- Crabmeat – 14 ounces
- Red grapefruit - 1
- Orange juice – 3 tbsp
- Sugar – 3 tbsp
- White vinegar – 2 tbsp
- Grated orange peel – 1 tsp
- Grated grapefruit peel – 1 tsp
- Mustard – ¼ cup

Directions

- Add water and salt in a pot and put neatly cut asparagus into it— cook for about 3-4 minutes.
- Peel the oranges and grapefruits. Cut them and remove the pits and segments.
- Mix all the fruits in a bowl with asparagus and half a cup of chives.
- Then place the crabmeat in the pot, and season with salt and pepper. Make sure everything coats each other.
- Now to prepare the dressing, mix the orange juice and grated peels along with sugar, vinegar, and mustard.
- Place the meaty mixture in the middle of lettuce leaves, and drizzle dressing over the salads.
- Serve.

Campanelle al Forno

Pairs with Chardonnay and Pinot Noir
Serves 2

Ingredients

- Lobster – 10 ounces
- Shallots – 2 tbsp
- Butter – 2 ounces
- White flour – ½ tsp
- Minced lemon zest – ¼ tsp
- Chopped parsley – 2 tbsp
- Chardonnay – 4 ounces
- Whipping cream – 16 ounces
- Chopped basil – 6 tbsp
- Lemon juice – 2 tsp

- Campanelle pasta – 4 ounces
- Breadcrumbs – 2 tbsp
- Parmesan cheese – 2 tbsp
- Sea salt – to taste
- Black pepper – to taste

Directions

- Preheat oven to 350 degrees.
- Boil salted water in a pot and cook pasta by following the package instructions.
- Cut the lobster into regular pieces. Add the chopped lobster, diced shallots, and butter in a saucepan and cook on medium-low heat for three minutes. Then, add zest, flour, and half of the parsley. Keep cooking for half a minute.
- Pour in the Chardonnay on medium-high heat to reduce the liquid by half.
- Combine lemon juice, basil, and cream. Allow the mixture to simmer for a couple of minutes to ensure it thickens.
- Mix the pasta and sauce and put handfuls of breadcrumbs on top with parmesan cheese. Bake it for 12-15 minutes.
- Serve.

Chapter 4
Sides and Dressings

When you sit in a restaurant and scan their menu, you are sure to see meat dishes filled with spices. It could be roasted chicken, beef lasagna, or crispy pork belly. For the side, you would consider salad or baked potato wedges. But you would not pay much attention to the side menu and the salad dressing, and that is where you're wrong!

Side dishes that accompany the main dish can make or break its overall taste. A specific dish should be combined with a side that complements the flavor of the main course and does not overpower or diminish it. A hearty beef dish would not go well with a rich, meaty side dish, whereas a light and fresh vegetable dish would work great with something heavy like cheese gratin.

If you have chosen lasagna, pairing it with a cheesy side will be overwhelming as it would fill you up fast. The side dish is what determines whether you would enjoy the flavor or even the texture of the food. Side dishes complete the meal, so every item needs to complement each other. They need to be ordered or prepared thoughtfully, according to your preferences but also the main dish. This is why food in itself is an art, and every item on a dining table needs to balance the other. Even during barbeques, not choosing the right side or eating meat without a side dish can completely change the barbeque experience. Side dishes are essential for barbeques because they diminish the heaviness of the meat and balance the oily and fatty taste with something light and fresh. Hence, every side dish at a barbeque is made up of vegetables, especially greens and carrots, giving the meal a nutritional edge.

Side dishes are also a great way to stay healthy and fit even if you eat greasy and calorie-rich foods. You can easily chop some vegetables and increase your intake of fiber and antioxidants, which shield your body from potential illnesses. Recipes of sides are simple to follow and easy to prepare. All you need is a fresh batch of vegetables or fruits and one or two other ingredients like cheese or bread.

Going for a side dish like salad means you must prepare the dressing for it as well, and you need to be careful with that. The ratio of the creaminess and tanginess of the dressing will decide the healthiness of the salad as well as its taste. Salads are meant to be light and wholesome, so drenching them with dressing is a mistake. The dressing is intended to boost the flavor of the ingredients and not overpower it. Often, salads are paired with unhealthy and oily dressings and balanced with heavy dishes, which means you can't have a nutritious meal anymore.

When preparing the dressing, include fewer egg yolks, mayonnaise, and sour cream. Use less oil and flavor it with vinegar and lemon. This way, the dressing will have fewer calories. The light nature of the salad adjusts well with a main course with meat, while salad is healthier to eat on its own as well.

It is important to pair a side and salad dressing with the correct dish, but it is also necessary to choose the right wine as well because even something as simple as a side dish and salad dressing can affect the wine's flavor.

Most of us are beginning to remove sides from the sidelines and consuming them on their own. This means that even these side dishes are now being paired with wines and choosing the right wine for each one is important. The way the side is prepared will help us pick out the right wine bottle.

As most sides consist of vegetables, let us consider a vegetable and wine pairing. If you are going for lighter vegetables, crisp white wine is the way to go. The method of preparation is vital, as well. Roasted or grilled vegetables complement bold wines while delicate cooking methods call for light wines.

A salad with a dressing that puts it at a higher acidic ratio should be paired with an acidic wine; pairing it with a wine with less acidity would corrupt the taste of the wine altogether. When it comes to creamy dressings, California Chardonnay is a great choice.

Once you begin to prepare food, keep two specific things in mind: a good wine pairing and a proper side dish will have you craving these sides as if they were the main course. My Skillet Green Beans and Potatoes are sure to be a hit with any entree, and my Honey Balsamic Vinaigrette and my Parmesan Salad Dressing will quickly become your go-to dressings of choice when you whip up some salad.

If you can't decide between which side dish to prepare, just make as many as you desire, and enjoy them as a meal as long as you have a good glass of Jenny Dawn Cellars wine to go along with it!

Recipes
Skillet Green Beans and Potatoes

Pairs with Pinot Noir
Serves 6

Ingredients

- Red potatoes – lbs
- Green beans – ¾ pounds
- Olive oil – 2 tbsp
- Cloves garlic– 2
- Salt – ¾ tsp
- Oregano – ½ tsp
- Sea salt – to taste
- Black pepper – to taste

Directions

- Peel of the potatoes and cut them in squares before adding them to a pot on high heat. Let the potatoes sit for five minutes or till they turn soft.
- Take a skillet and cook minced garlic with olive oil. Drain the boiled potatoes then add them into the skillet.
- After a couple of minutes, add in green beans. Keep cooking until they turn soft.
- Sprinkle the seasoning on top and saute for a minute or two.
- Serve.

Goat Cheese Stuffed Figs

Pairs with Chardonnay
Serves 6

Ingredients

- Dried figs - 18
- Goat cheese – 3 ounces
- Bacon – 4 slices
- Honey– 1-2 tbsp

Directions

- Slice the figs and top with ½ tsp of goat cheese.

- Cook the bacon till it turns crispy and brown. Take a kitchen knife, cut the bacon into pieces, and place it on top of the figs.
- Put the finished product on a plate and drizzle honey on top.
- Serve.

Honey Balsamic Vinaigrette

Ingredients

- Balsamic vinegar – 3 tbsp
- Extra virgin olive oil – 3 tbsp
- Chopped shallots – 1 tbsp
- Honey – 1 tsp
- Water – 1 tsp
- Sea salt to taste – to taste
- Ground black pepper – to taste

Directions

- Combine all ingredients in a jar and shake thoroughly before serving.

Parmesan Salad Dressing

Ingredients

- Honey – 1 tbsp
- Red wine vinegar – 1/3 cup
- Extra virgin olive oil – 2/3 cup
- Garlic cloves – 3
- Parmesan cheese – ½ cup
- Italian parsley -1/4 cup
- Red pepper flakes – ½ tsp
- Garlic powder – ¼ tsp
- Sea salt – to taste

Directions

- Chop parsley and garlic cloves, and grate the parmesan cheese finely.
- Combine all ingredients in a jar and shake thoroughly before serving.

Shaved Fennel and Avocado Salad

Pairs with Chardonnay and Union Station

Ingredients

- Fennel heads – 2
- Avocados – 2
- Ruby-red grapefruits– 2
- Macadamia nuts – ½ cup
- Fennel fronds, chopped – 2 tbsp
- Minced shallot – ½
- Juice and zest of 1 lemon
- Juice and zest of 1 orange
- Rice wine vinegar – 1 tsp
- Olive oil – 1 cup
- Sugar – 1 cup
- Water – 1 cup

- Mache, roots removed – 2 cups
- Salt – to taste
- White pepper – to taste

Directions

- Pour water along with sugar in a saucepan. Bring it to boil, remove from heat, and place it in the refrigerator.
- Remove the sections and the skin of the grapefruit. Let them rest in a bowl and mix in the syrup made earlier. Refrigerate after coating with syrup.
- Mix the shallots and vinegar with the zest and juices. Add in the seasoning, then refrigerate.
- Shave the fennel, chop it thoroughly, and toss them in as well. Mix some chopped fennel fronds along with some seasoning as well. Also, add vinaigrette in the bowl. Stir the mixture well.
- Take the avocado halves from the skin, and put each half on one plate. Place the dressed fennel on top of the halves— dust the chopped macadamia nuts on top of each plate.
- Allocate grapefruit sections for each plate. Place mache on the plates and drizzle with vinaigrette.
- Serve.

Grilled Portobello Mushrooms

Pairs with Pinot Noir

Ingredients

- Portobello mushrooms – 3
- Canola oil – ¼ cup
- Onion – 3 tbsp
- Minced garlic cloves – 4
- Balsamic vinegar – 4 tbsp

Directions

- Mix oil, chopped garlic, chopped onions, and vinegar in a bowl.
- Wash the mushrooms and place their caps on a plate. Remove the stems.

- Pour the mixture over the caps. Allow them to sit for an hour.
- Heat a grill and place the mushroom caps on it for about 8-10 minutes. Keep grilling till they look brown and ready.
- Serve.

Chapter 5
Desserts

Desserts are a must after finishing a meal. They are perfect for topping off a savory meal on a sweet note. After consuming a spread packed with meat, cheese, or vegetables, everyone wants dessert. Whether it is molten lava cake oozing with chocolate and with vanilla ice cream on the side, a syrupy pudding that jiggles as you cut through it, or a piece of moist red velvet cake topped with whipped cream, you simply cannot decline the offer for dessert.

Desserts keep us happy. Sugar is known to improve mood and release chemicals responsible for satisfaction and contentment.

However, you should not have desserts every day because excessive sugar can lead to chronic illnesses like obesity and diabetes. Anything consumed without moderation will turn out to be harmful to the body.

But then, desserts can also be healthy for you because you can always add fruits to it. Some desserts have sizeable portions of raspberries, blueberries, blackberries, and, most commonly, strawberries. Berries are considered some of the healthiest food in the world; they are loaded with nutrients and minerals that help strengthen the body and shield it from dangerous illnesses. They are packed with antioxidants that prevent cell damage. They are high in fiber, which plays a vital role in regulating the digestive system and abundant in vitamin C, which protects one against cardiovascular diseases.

Many desserts are also made from dark chocolate, which prevents heart diseases and lowers blood pressure. Dark chocolate is also an amazing alternative for people who prefer their desserts to be on the bitter or bitter-sweet side. It can even be an excellent dessert for diabetic patients if kept unsweetened. In general, dark chocolate gives a healthier kick to desserts, and pairing it with fruits makes the combination even better.

The calories in the cream cheese or powdered sugar that you add in a dessert can be balanced by the wholesome qualities of dark chocolate and a bit of fruit. Desserts are easier to prepare as the ingredients are typically straightforward. The only concern is to keep the temperature right. You can whip up a creamy trifle or a blueberry pie with ingredients that are already stocked in your pantry. You only have to heat them in the oven at the right time. Take it out once it's done to perfection, and indulge in that sweet goodness. The taste of a dessert and its sweetness, or even bitterness for that matter, can be enhanced by pairing it with a glass of wine that balances the flavors out. The darker the dessert gets, the darker the wine needs to be. If you pair a glass of white wine with dark-chocolate buttery brownie, the flavor won't match.

When it comes to pairing, it is better to choose a fruity dessert with an acidic wine as the dessert is acidic itself. A sweet dish needs to be paired with an even sweeter wine. Make sure that your pick of wine is generally on the sweeter side, and matches the color, intensity, and flavor of the dessert on the whole. Keep this in mind, and you wouldn't face difficulty in choosing the wine that would go well with buttery shortbread cookies or chocolate trifle.

There is always room for dessert, but then again, there's always room for wine as well. So properly pairing both wouldn't leave room for any other cravings! Just pour yourself a glass of Riesling and pair it with my Honey Soaked Figs. Of course, my Lemon Blueberry Clafoutis is a lovely treat, but you will make it even more special if you enjoy it with a bottle of Jenny Dawn Cellars Wichita Moments wine.

Go crazy with these dessert recipes! Make one for breakfast or even at 1 in the night when you cannot fall asleep and are bored out of your mind. These moist, sweet, and fruity desserts are perfect for any time and occasion.

Recipes
Spiced Poached Pears

Pairs with Chardonnay or Wichita Moments
Serves 6

Ingredients

- Pears - 6
- Pinot noir – 1
- Vanilla bean, split in half -1
- Cinnamon sticks – 2
- Bay leaves – 2
- Sugar – 2 cups

- Containers of mascarpone cheese – 2 of 8 ounces
- Heavy cream – ½ cup
- Pinch of cinnamon
- Powdered sugar – ½ cup
- Butter – 2 tbsp

Direction

- Simmer wine in a saucepan. Add cinnamon sticks, bay leaves, vanilla bean, and sugar to the pan.
- Combine some peeled pears as well, make sure they're cut in two.
- Let the mixture heat for about 15-20 minutes.
- Set it aside after removing from heat.
- Mix heavy cream, powdered sugar, cheese, and cinnamon in a bowl. After removing the pears from the wine, scoop up the creamy mixture and fill the two halves of the pear.
- Heat the rest of the wine mixture to reduce it by half, and combine butter to give it a velvety touch.
- Pour it over the cream stuffed pears and serve.

Lemon Blueberry Clafoutis

Pairs with Wichita Passion or Sweet Red Wine
Serves 4

Ingredients

- Blueberries – 2 cups
- Castor sugar– ½ cup and 3-4 tsp
- Cubes of cream cheese– 4 ounces
- All-purpose flour – ¼ cup
- Vanilla – 1 tsp
- Eggs– 3
- Whole milk – ½ cup
- Powdered sugar – 1 tbsp
- Zest of 1 lemon

Directions

- Preheat oven to 400 degrees.
- Combine cubes of cream cheese, half a cup of caster sugar, flour, one egg, and vanilla with a mixer till it's smooth and creamy.
- Add the rest of the eggs to the mixture as well. Blend till everything combines together. Pour in milk slowly while mixing at the same time.
- Butter dessert dishes and dust leftover castor sugar.
- Place half a cup of blueberries in each of the dishes. Add the batter to each dish, topping with some lemon zest.
- Bake for 20 minutes or till the desserts become golden. After removing, let them cool, and sprinkle some powdered sugar on top.
- Serve.

Honey Soaked Figs

Pairs with Riesling
Serves 2

Ingredients

- Dried figs - 6
- Honey – 2 tbsp
- Extra virgin olive oil – 1 tbsp
- Water – 1 tbsp
- Mascarpone cheese – 1 tbsp
- Thyme – 1 tsp

Directions

- Pour honey, oil, and water in a pan and let the mixture simmer.
- Add in figs and place a lid on the pan. Keep the figs stay for a couple of minutes.

- Settle the figs in a plate and drizzle a bit of honey on top. Top the figs with mascarpone cheese.
- Place thyme on the dish to complete.
- Serve.

Strawberry Balsamic Crostini

Pairs with Red Caboose and Rosé Wine
Serves 4

Ingredients

- Fresh strawberries – 1 pint
- Cream cheese – 1 cup
- Basil leaves – 2 tbsp
- Chives – 1 tbsp
- French baguette – 1
- Balsamic vinegar – 3 tbsp
- Honey – ¼ cup
- Sea Salt– to taste
- Black pepper – to taste

Directions

- Chop basil leaves and chives and combine with cream cheese in a mixing bowl.
- Broil the bread for a couple of minutes to lightly toast the sides.
- Spread the cream cheese mixture and sliced strawberries on top of the bread.
- Drizzle honey and vinegar, lightly seasoning at the same time.
- Serve.

Chapter 6
Vegan

Vegan food has been rapidly gaining popularity all over the world because of its impressive health benefits. Even though people love to stereotype vegan food to be unappetizing or nothing but leafy, green veggies, but that is never the case! Not only is it rich with nutrients, but you can also turn any vegan dish into a mouth-watering experience through the right recipe.

There are plenty of vegan dishes to choose from. You can enjoy a light and savory cauliflower steak, crisped to perfection, and sprinkled with a generous amount of garnished vegetables. This is a meat alternative that has even die-heart meat-lovers drooling. On the other hand, you also have vegan chocolate chip cookies, which are gooey chocolate centered. They are crunchy at first but melt in your mouth as you begin to chew.

So vegan food can be prepared in heavenly ways and do the original dishes justice. At the same time, it is packed with health benefits, which are enough to rid any risks of chronic illnesses or concerns. Fruits and vegetables are the staples of vegan food. There are also whole grains, legumes, seeds, and nuts included in the mix as well.

Most of these foods are great sources of fiber, minerals, vitamins C and E, and iron. Therefore veganism is considered as a good diet for reducing the probability of developing diabetes, hypertension, obesity, or heart diseases. Veganism can also help reduce weight because vegan food has low calories and consists of less saturated fats.

This does not mean that you should completely compromise on the meaty dishes and dairy products which rule the food market. Keep everything balanced, and there is nothing to overthink. If you want to indulge in the flavorful world of meat, just include a couple of vegetables and grains on the side to ensure you are not overdoing on the bad cholesterol.

Also, more and more people are leaning towards veganism to improve their health, even if it is not for the long-term. The trend in plant-based meat has taken the world by storm. Massive restaurant chains are also including or contemplating to include plant-based meat to their menu lists. So even non-vegan people are trying these options out occasionally to increase their intake of healthy food.

Though vegan food is flavorful and healthy, it tastes almost extraordinary when paired with the correct wine. There is no doubt that wine is a mind-blowing alcoholic beverage which can change the taste and experience of every dish in existence. Choosing the right wine will determine whether your experience of preparing vegan enchiladas for your friends will leave them dissatisfied or craving for more.

If you are a vegan, you might need to consider a wine that is vegan-friendly as well. Once again, it is important to keep the nature of wine in mind when pairing. Grilled food tastes scrumptious when paired with Chardonnay. If the wine is full-bodied, pairing it with a light vegan dish with fewer sauces or just with a simple side takes away the flavor of the wine.

Higher-tannin red wines tend to complement rich food well as the flavors from both sides have space to balance. Beans go quite well with sparkling or rose wine, while root vegetables are complemented with full-bodied white wines. Legumes should be paired with earthy red wines like Pinot Noir. You might feel confused about the pairing and just cannot wait to dig your fork into the meal and pop the cork of your wine bottle. So, in that case, leave the brainstorming be and just go for a rose wine, which is incredible with most foods.

This Vegan Enchiladas recipe will make you feel the same. You will want to grab a nearby Jenny Dawn Cellars Pinot Noir quickly, and just gorge on the vegan goodness before you. This scrumptious dish is sure to be loved by all vegans and non-vegans alike!

Recipes
Vegan Enchiladas

Pairs with Pinot Noir

Ingredients to Prepare Crema

- Raw cashews – 1 cup
- Lime juice – 2 tbsp
- White vinegar – 1 tsp
- Paprika – 1 tsp
- Salt – ½ tsp

Ingredients to Prepare the Sauce

- Tomatillos – 2 pounds
- Onion – 1
- Garlic cloves – 2
- Jalapeno – 1

- Vegetable stock – 2 cups
- Cilantro – ½ cup
- Salt and pepper to taste

Ingredients to Prepare Enchiladas

- Butternut squash – 2 cups
- Olive oil – 2 tbsp
- Onion – 1
- Shallots – 2
- Shiitake caps – 2 cups
- Corn – 2 cups
- Kale – 2 cups
- Canola oil – 1 cup
- Tortillas – 12
- Salt and pepper to taste.

Crema Preparation

- Take cashews in a bowl and pour in hot water.
- Cover the cashews. Set the bowl aside for 2 hours.
- After draining, put the cashews in a food processor.
- Then, add in the rest of the ingredients.

Sauce Preparation

- Place saucepan on the stove. Put the onion, garlic, stock, jalapeno, and tomatillos inside the saucepan.
- After the vegetables turn soft, place them in a food processor along with the cilantro and seasoning.

- Turn on the processor and let the mixture turn into a paste.

Enchilada Preparation

- Take a huge skillet and drizzle a tbsp of oil into it. Cook the shallots and onions on the skillet till they turn soft and brown.
- Add in the shiitake, then add corn— cook for a few minutes. Then, add the kale.
- Lather squash pieces with oil and sprinkle seasoning. Roast them in the oven for a good 12-15 minutes. Mix the squash with the kale. Make sure you season with salt and pepper.
- Add canola oil in a skillet. Put a tortilla in the oil and cook for a couple of seconds. Continue to do the same for the rest of the tortillas.
- Place the tortillas in a baking dish. First, smother the tomatillo sauce on the dish, then fill the tortillas with the sauce. After lining the tortillas up on the dish, spread some of the sauce on the top as well.
- Bake the dish till the enchiladas are cooked thoroughly, and serve.

Chapter 7
Wine Tips

"Wine, to me, is passion. It's family and friends. It's the warmth of heart and generosity of spirit. Wine is art. It's culture. It's the essence of civilization and the art of living."

-Robert Mondavi

I have been a wine drinker for 16 years now. Finishing my day with a shiny glass of dark-red or silvery-white wine has been a regular for me at this point. As I have invested such a significant portion of my life to wine, I am often asked about which wine I prefer the most. Sometimes I feel like the answer might be at the tip of my tongue, while more often, I simply cannot choose just one favorite wine as I like them all.

It is the same as asking a mother to choose a favorite child, a question no mother can answer swiftly. Once I dived into the world of wine, I realized how every dish we eat and every flavor that graces our tongue connects with the texture, flavor, and acidity of the wine. So, I began to picture a specific wine in my head, even before I began to cook. The thing is, wine is a special drink, and it is an art. It has a rich history with each event unfolding to describe how this beautiful creation took the world by the collar and shook it to its core. As a winemaker and individual spending years and years experimenting with the alcoholic beverage, I have a few tips to share regarding wine. These serve both as facts and tips, but they are things about wine which I learned after beginning my own winery:

Prominent Jenny Dawn Cellars Grapes and Wine Regions

I make sure I source grapes from some of the finest growers in the nation for my winery Jenny Dawn Cellars. It was hard work at first and took me quite a lot of time and searching to find the perfectly fitting grapes for my wine. But the process was worth it without a doubt. For fruit wine, the winery has used apples, blackberries and watermelon, which are sourced from Kansas to prepare the Wichita Moments, Wichita Passion and Rosé wines.

When it comes to grape wine, the Jenny Dawn Cellars lovely Chardonnay is sourced from Sonoma Valley, Pinot Noir from Russian River Valley, Cabernet Sauvignon, and

Sweet Red Wine from Paso Robles. The Black Locomotive uses Crimson Cabernet grapes, Union Station uses Chardonnay and the Red Caboose is a rosé from Crimson Cabernet. The grapes from these wines were all sourced from Kansas. I love these wines to death, not only because they are flavorful and tasty, but also because they were sourced from the best! The 2018 Chardonnay from my winery is a classic. It is bright, fresh, and acidic with a yellow straw color. It is dominated by green apple, pear, and zesty citrus notes. The Chardonnay is smooth on the palate, nicely textured with a lively finish. In the vineyard, this Chardonnay was handpicked after fully ripening, and then it was brought to the winery for gentle pressing.

The juice was fermented on 85% neutral French oak and 15% new French oak. After primary fermentation was complete, the young wine continued to age in contact with the yeast lees stirring every few weeks. During aging, a quarter of the wine then underwent a secondary, malolactic fermentation to soften the natural acidity and add complexity. The wine was bottled on December 3, 2019, at our urban winery in Wichita, KS. Our 2017 Pinot Noir is also expressive on the palate with flavors of cranberry, cherry, and raspberries with a lush red color. It is filled with fruit but also has an earthy undertone that brings exceptional balance to the wine. On the palate, the flavor and texture is of deeply layered fruit and fine tannins.

In the vineyard, this Pinot Noir was handpicked, and it was all cluster pressed in the winery. The juice, skins, must, and seeds went through native fermentation in stainless steel, undergoing three delicate punch-downs a day. After primary fermentation was complete, it was transferred to neutral French oak for aging.

Our 2017 Cabernet Sauvignon is aromatic with flavors of black cherry, pomegranate, currant, black pepper, plum, and blackberry. The wine is also complemented by dark chocolate and tobacco leaf with a deep ruby red color. Rounding out the nose are aromas of black olives and dried thyme.

This wine is bold and assertive, with complexity and depth. It also has a purity of fruit and subtle layers of flavors and texture that harmonize and enhance. In the vineyard, these cab grapes were machine harvested, then in the winery, all the juice was fermented in stainless steel. 85% of the wine was aged in neutral French oak, while 15% of the wine was aged in new French oak. Our 2017 Sweet Red Wine is packed with flavors of sweet oak, espresso, black cherry, pomegranate, currant, and black pepper. The wine has a finesse of dried plum and savory sage with an opaque deep purple color. It leaves soft tannins to linger on the palate with caramel, fudge, and vanilla to the finish.

Again, these cab grapes were machine harvested in the vineyard. The juice is then fermented in stainless steel within the winery. Similarly, to the previous wine, 85% of the wine was aged in neutral French oak, while the other 15% was aged in new French oak.

Our 2015 Riesling has pronounced flavors of apricot, honeysuckle, nectarine, and spiced pears with acidity in perfect balance. The wine is golden yellow in color with a light to medium body with fair amounts of sweetness but not overpowering.

The cool climate of Lake County, North Coast was perfect for the grapes to have a long ripening on the vine necessary to produce a botrytis rot. In the vineyard, the Riesling grapes dimpled and became high in sugar. In the winery, the grapes were basket pressed with a lot of pressure and fermented in stainless steel. Our 2019 Union Station wine is made from Kansas Chardonnay grapes. It is dry, crisp, light bodied, straw or pale yellow in color, with aromas and flavors of lime peel, Asian pear, citrus blossom, and limestone.

Our 2019 Black Locomotive wine is made from Kansas Crimson Cabernet grapes. Crimson Cabernet is a hybrid. It combines the grapes of Cabernet Sauvignon and Norton. This wine is ruby red, almost purple in color, dry, medium bodied, robust, and has lush fruits like black cherry and elderberry with delicate fig. It also has basil, and cedar spices.

Our 2019 Red Caboose is made by using the saignée method from Kansas Crimson Cabernet grapes. This wine is light red in color. It is dry, delicate, slightly fruity, and savory. It has aromas and flavors of cranberry, banana, roses, and lilies. Our Rosé Wine can be enjoyed on its own and it is perfect for patio sipping.

Our 2019 Rosé Wine is made from watermelons grown in Kansas. It is a beautiful pink color with a sweet, fruity, and slightly tart flavor. It has aromas and flavors of honeydew, cantaloupe, watermelon, dandelion, and green grass. Our Rosé Wine is sweet goodness in a glass.

The Art and Science of Drinking Wine

There are about 10,000 different varieties of grapes in the world used in the making of wine. I was astonished by this figure. It's just a fruit yet consists of so many different types with evidently unique flavors or tastes. This pushed me to dig a little deep, so I began to study to become a certified sommelier through the Master Court.

The Master Court of Sommeliers was established in 1977. Its purpose is to provide the ultimate experience in beverage service. Though the concept seems intriguing and even entertaining, the process of becoming a certified sommelier takes a lot of time. The competition is quite fierce.

Apparently, in North America, only a portion of 149 professionals have been able to receive the highest honor of becoming a Master Sommelier. This number includes 125 men and only 24 women. After devoting my life to wine, my goal is to become a Master someday.

That is nothing but a sweet, short dream of mine, but you do not need to be a wine connoisseur or a master sommelier to appreciate the art and science of wine tasting!

When I talk about wine in general, it consists of five basic steps – steps which even you can master: appearance, aroma, body, taste, and finish.

Appearance – The appearance is not only the simple outwardly color of the wine but also the clarity of the wine. You can check the appearance of the wine by tilting the glass and examining whether the wine is clear or hazy. These can even help in telling the acidity and filtration of the wine.

Aroma – The aroma of wine is just as the name suggests – the overall smell of the drink. There is no one specific kind of aroma. There are fruity, earthy, citrusy, etc. To inhale the smell of the wine, swirl the drink in the glass and then bring it to your nose. Make sure the wine is swirled properly instead of just rotating the glass lightly.

Body – The body of a wine is whether the wine feels light or heavy upon drinking it. The more weight or full-bodied the wine, the more it'll fill up your mouth. Wines can come in all bodies, such as light, medium, and last but not least, full-bodied.

Taste – The way wine is prepared to the way it is poured into the glass - everything affects the taste of the wine. You must be familiar with its different aromas and how long the flavor of the wine lingers in your mouth to know what it takes for the wine to taste fine. Looking at the color of the wine also helps determine the taste of the drink. For instance, if the wine is darker, it is more flavorful.

Finish – the finish of a wine is the taste of the drink staying on your palate after you've already gulped the luscious goodness. This is more like the aftertaste of the wine, proving whether the wine is of good-quality –healthy – or not.

I love drinking wine because wine converts every meal into an occasion. It makes every table more elegant and every day more civilized. Now that you know the basics of the art and science of tasting wine, you can drink wine like the sommeliers.

Cheers and let your wine moment begin!

Expanding Your Palate Through Wineucation

Every wine lover wants to expand their palate and understand how to use their taste buds to savor the wine better. You must have sharp senses to taste the wine fully.

Before beginning to taste the wine and letting it rest on your palate, make sure that you're in a place without any distractions.

Then, inspect the wine by keeping it under good lighting, and bring it close to your nose and take in a good whiff. After noticing the viscosity and color of the wine and taking in the smells, taste the wine. In this stage, you'll taste whether the wine is sweet or on the acidic side. You should also keep the wine's texture in mind.

Try to notice where you feel the tannin from the wine in your mouth – the roof, side, or the middle? Now, once you keep practicing whether the wine tasted a tad bit too acidic or sweet, you'll begin to identify flavors. This, in turn, will help expand your palate and allow you to become a better judge of wines!

Wine Storage and Aging

The duration of storing the wine along with the place it is locked up in also determines the taste of the wine. Here are a couple of things to keep in mind about the wine storing and the aging process:

Store the Wine in A Dark Place

Keeping the wines in a dim place prevents UV rays from hitting the wine bottle. As more light hits the wine bottles, it makes the wines smell foul, which ultimately affects the taste as well. The light reacts to the drink and creates a rotten-egg smell. Also, a dark place helps the drink stay in a more humid environment, which keeps it healthy.

Positioning the Wine Correctly

The way the wine is positioned can also have an effect on the development of the wine. Years of wine preparation shows that wine should be placed horizontally as that doesn't let the cork turn dry. This is also why it is preferred to keep the wines in humid conditions, so the cork of the bottle is damp.

Placing the Wine in a Cool Place

Wine should be stored in the perfect temperature, and this means not just any place that is dark or could be humid. It needs to be placed somewhere cool rather than of varying temperatures. If the temperature is too warm, it can have a direct effect on the taste of the wine because it cooks the wine, which gives it a rather sour flavor.

Wine Glasses

The shape of the wine glasses and the way you tilt it in the air before drinking the contents can also drastically change the flavor of the wine. You drink wine by tilting the glass in different ways because of the shape of the glass. If the wine glass has a narrow rim, you will lean your head back to sip.

This alters the way the drink comes in contact with your tongue. The wine hits the different portions of your tongue like the front, back, or sides, and that changes its taste altogether because of the different receptors on the tongue. The Bordeaux glass has a larger rim opening, so it allows the wine to go forth all at one go. This compels the acidity of the wine to be diluted, which makes the wine taste fruitier and smoother while a wine glass with a smaller opening pushes the wine to hit one point, which then spreads around as you keep drinking. This can cause the wine to taste more acidic and stronger.

Decanting Wine

Decanting wine is the process of pouring wine from the bottle to another vessel; usually, a glass container. As you pour the contents in the vessel, it separates the sediment in the wine. If the sediment stays, gives the wine a bitterer flavor. Also, transferring the wine to the decanter also helps the wine breathe and come to life. When choosing a decanter or vessel to transfer your wine, make sure that it is squeaky-clean and does not have any lingering foul aromas.

Even if you don't want to expand your palate and taste wine like a pro, you can still drink wine as a means of comforting yourself after a long day. That is what I do! Though I am a professional winemaker and can taste the texture and flavor of wine in a heartbeat, I still like to pour a glass for myself just for the fun of it all. But keeping these wine tips in mind can inform you about the different ways to enjoy wine, and make the process of drinking wine with your favorite dish even better!

www.ingramcontent.com/pod-product-compliance
Lightning Source LLC
Chambersburg PA
CBHW070054100426
42740CB00013B/2840
* 9 7 8 1 9 5 2 2 6 3 5 4 5 *